WILDLIFE VIEWING AREAS

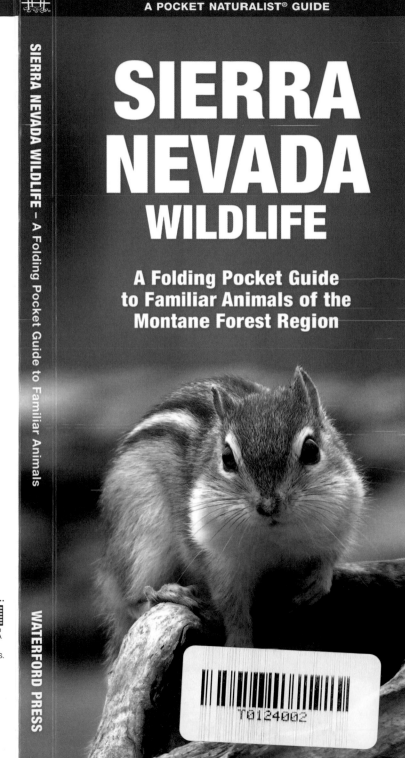

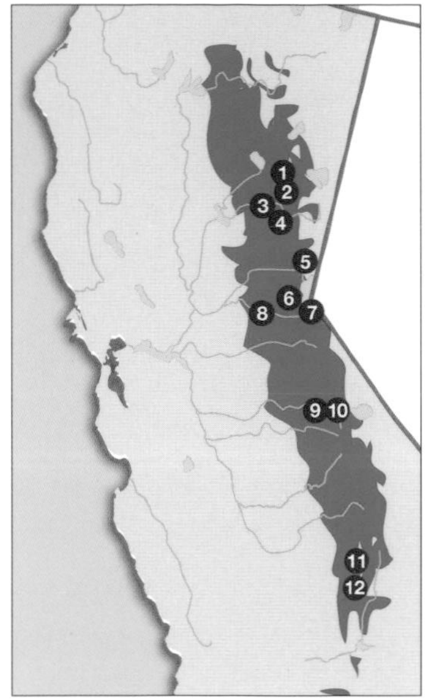

1. Antelope Lake
2. Lake Davis
3. Sand Pond
4. Jackson Meadow Reservoir
5. Martis Creek Lake
6. Emerald Bay & D.L. Bliss State Parks
7. Taylor Creek Visitor Center
8. Sly Park Recreation Area
9. Yosemite National Park
10. Tioga Lake
11. Kings Canyon National Park
12. Sequoia National Park

The longest continuous mountain chain in the US, the Sierra Nevada mountains are one of the most diverse coniferous forests on Earth. The Sierran Montane forest occurs in three main regions at different elevations. The elevations at which these regions occur differ on the western and eastern side of the range due to precipitation, which is much greater on the western side.

The Lower Montane Forest

- 3,000-7,000 ft. (900-2100 m) West
- 7,000-9,000 ft. (2100-2700 m) East
- Indicator species include ponderosa pine, Jeffrey pine, black oak, sugar pine, incense-cedar, white fir and giant sequoia.

The Upper Montane Forest

- 7,000-9,000 ft. (2100-2700 m) West
- 9,000-10,500 ft. (2700-3200 m) East
- Indicator species include lodgepole pine, red fir and western juniper.

Subalpine Forest

- 9,000-11,000 ft. (2700-3300 m) West
- 10,500-12,000 ft. (3200-3600 m) East
- Indicator species include whitebark pine, western white pine, mountain hemlock and lodgepole pine.

Most illustrations show the adult male in breeding coloration. Colors and markings may be duller or absent during different seasons. The measurements denote the length of species from nose/bill to tail tip. Butterfly measurements denote wingspan. Illustrations are not to scale.

Made in the USA

Waterford Press publishes reference guides that introduce readers to nature observation, outdoor recreation and survival skills. Product information is featured on the website: **www.waterfordpress.com**

Text & illustrations © 2013, 2023 Waterford Press Inc. All rights reserved.
Photos © iStock Photo. To order or for information on custom published products, please call 800-434-2555 or email orderdesk@waterfordpress.com. For permissions or to share comments, email editor@waterfordpress.com.

ISBN 978-1-58355-795-2 $7.95 U.S.
50795
9 781583 557952
UPC 8 84682 01103 1
10 9 8 7 6 5 4 3 2 1
2309335

SIERRA NEVADA WILDLIFE – A Folding Pocket Guide to Familiar Animals

WATERFORD PRESS

A POCKET NATURALIST® GUIDE

SIERRA NEVADA WILDLIFE

A Folding Pocket Guide to Familiar Animals of the Montane Forest Region

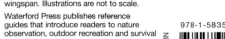

T0124002

BUTTERFLIES & MOTHS

Western Tiger Swallowtail
Papilio rutulus
To 4 in. (10 cm)

Pipevine Swallowtail
Battus philenor
To 3.5 in. (9 cm)

Pale Tiger Swallowtail
Papilio eurymedon
To 4 in. (10 cm)

California Tortoiseshell
Nymphalis californica
To 2 in. (5 cm)

Sara Orangetip
Anthocharis sara
To 1.5 in. (4 cm)

California Sister
Adelpha californica
To 3.5 in. (9 cm)

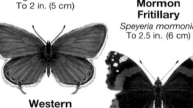

Milbert's Tortoiseshell
Aglais milberti
To 2 in. (5 cm)

Mormon Fritillary
Speyeria mormonia
To 2.5 in. (6 cm)

Monarch
Danaus plexippus
To 4 in. (10 cm)

Western Tailed Blue
Cupido amyntula
To 1.25 in. (3.2 cm)

Red Admiral
Vanessa atalanta
To 2.5 in. (6 cm)

Hoary Comma
Polygonia gracilis
To 1.5 in. (4 cm)

Buckeye
Junonia coenia
To 2.5 in. (6 cm)

Riding's Forester
Alypia ridingsi
To 1 in. (3 cm)

Bumblebee Moth
Hemaris diffinis
To 2 in. (5 cm)
Distinguished by clear wings and furry body.

Ceanothus Silk Moth
Hyalophora euryalus
To 4.5 in. (11 cm)

INVERTEBRATES

Common Whitetail
Libellula lydia
To 2 in. (5 cm)

Vivid Dancer
Argia vivida
To 1.5 in. (4 cm)

Green Darner
Anax junius
To 3 in. (8 cm)

Flame Skimmer
Libellula saturata
To 2 in. (5 cm)

Western Black Widow ♀
Latrodectus hesperus
To .5 in. (1.3 cm)
Has red hourglass marking on abdomen. Venomous.

Ichneumon Wasp
Ophion spp.
To .75 in. (1.9 cm)

Goldenrod Crab Spider
Misumena vatia
To .4 in. (1 cm)

Black-and-yellow Garden Spider ♀
Argiope aurantia
To 1.25 in. (3.2 cm)

Golden Buprestid
Buprestis aurulenta
To .8 in. (2 cm)

Black Flies
Simulium spp.
To .1 in. (.3 cm)
Tiny humpbacked biting flies.

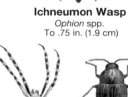

Yellow Jacket
Vespula spp.
To .6 in. (1.5 cm)
Aggressive picnic pest can sting repeatedly.

Diving Beetle
Dytiscus spp.
To 1.5 in. (4 cm)
Swims by using its hind legs like oars.

Water Strider
Gerris remigis
To .5 in. (1.3 cm)
"Skates" on the surface of quiet waters.

Actual Size

Wood Tick
Dermacentor spp.
To .25 in. (.6 cm)
Feeds on blood and transmits diseases.

Deer Fly
Chrysops spp.
To 0.6 in. (1.5 cm)
Females feed on the blood of mammals and deliver a painful bite.

Whirligig Beetle
Family Gyrinidae
To .5 in. (1.3 cm)
Large swarms swirl around on the water's surface.

FISHES

Many of these species have been widely introduced in lakes and rivers.

Rainbow Trout
Oncorhynchus mykiss To 44 in. (1.1 m)

Golden Trout
Oncorhynchus aguabonita
To 28 in. (70 cm)

Cutthroat Trout
Oncorhynchus clarkii To 39 in. (98 cm)
Told by red mark near throat.

Brook Trout
Salvelinus fontinalis To 28 in. (70 cm)
Reddish side spots have blue halos.

Green Sunfish
Lepomis cyanellus
To 12 in. (30 cm)

Bluegill
Lepomis macrochirus
To 16 in. (40 cm)

Pumpkinseed
Lepomis gibbosus
To 16 in. (40 cm)

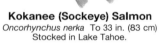

Kokanee (Sockeye) Salmon
Oncorhynchus nerka To 33 in. (83 cm)
Stocked in Lake Tahoe.

Lake Trout
Salvelinus namaycush To 4 ft. (1.2 m)
Dark fish is covered in light spots. Tail is deeply forked.

Largemouth Bass
Micropterus salmoides To 40 in. (1 m)

Brown Bullhead
Ameiurus nebulosus To 20 in. (50 cm)

REPTILES & AMPHIBIANS

Sierra Nevada Yellow-legged Frog
Rana sierrae
To 3.5 in. (9 cm)
Undersides are yellowish. Does not call.

Pacific Treefrog
Pseudacris regilla
To 2 in. (5 cm)
Color ranges from brown to green. Note dark eye stripe. Call is 2-part – *kreck-ek* – with the last syllable rising.

California Red-legged Frog
Rana aurora draytoni
To 5 in. (13 cm)
Underside of legs are reddish. Call is a stuttering series of gutteral growls.

REPTILES & AMPHIBIANS

Western Toad
Anaxyrus boreas
To 4 in. (10 cm)
Note cream-colored dorsal stripe. Males have a soft, clucking call.

Bullfrog
Lithobates catesbeianus
To 8 in. (20 cm)
Large frog has a rounded snout. Call is a deep-pitched – *jurrrooom*.

California Toad
Anaxyrus boreas halophilus
To 4 in. (10 cm)
Males have a soft, clucking call.

California Slender Salamander
Batrachoseps attenuatus To 6 in. (15 cm)
Worm-like species has tiny limbs.

California Tiger Salamander
Ambystoma californiense
To 9 in. (23 cm)

Western Pond Turtle
Clemmys marmorata
To 7 in. (18 cm)

Sierra Newt
Taricha torosa sierrae To 8 in. (20 cm)
Red-brown skin is warty.

Western Whiptail
Aspidoscelis tigris To 12 in. (30 cm)
Back and sides are dark-spotted. Note long tail.

Western Fence Lizard
Sceloporus occidentalis
To 9 in. (23 cm)

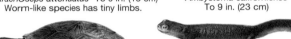

Sierra Mountain Kingsnake
Lampropeltis zonata To 40 in. (1 m)

Western Skink
Plestiodon skiltonianus To 9 in. (23 cm)
Has 4 light body stripes.

Western Terrestrial Garter Snake
Thamnophis elegans elegans
To 40 in. (1 m)

California Kingsnake
Lampropeltis getula californiae
To 7 ft. (2.1 m)

Rubber Boa
Charina bottae To 33 in. (83 cm)
Glossy, stout gray to brown snake.

Northern Pacific Rattlesnake
Crotalus oreganus oreganus
To 4 ft. (1.2 m)
Venomous.

Pacific Gopher Snake
Pituophis catenifer catenifer
To 8 ft. (2.4 m)
Non-venomous snake mimics a rattlesnake when threatened.

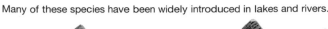

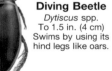

Dusky Grouse
Dendragapus obscurus
To 21 in. (53 cm)
During breeding season,
males hoot loudly
to attract females.

Mountain Quail
Oreortyx pictus
To 12 in. (30 cm)
Note straight
head plume.

Band-tailed Pigeon
Patagioenas fasciata
To 15 in. (38 cm)
Note white crescent
on nape.

Golden Eagle
Aquila chrysaetos
To 40 in. (1 m)

Peregrine Falcon
Falco peregrinus
To 20 in. (50 cm)

Bald Eagle
Haliaeetus leucocephalus
To 40 in. (1 m)

American Kestrel
Falco sparverius
To 12 in. (30 cm)

Great Horned Owl
Bubo virginianus
To 25 in. (63 cm)
Call is a resonant –
hoo-HOO-hoooo.

Great Gray Owl
Strix nebulosa
To 33 in. (83 cm)
Large gray owl has
a black and white
"bow tie."

Acorn Woodpecker
Melanerpes formicivorus
To 10 in. (25 cm)

Downy Woodpecker
Dryobates pubescens
To 6 in. (15 cm)
The similar hairy
woodpecker is larger
and has a longer bill.

White-headed Woodpecker
Picoides albolarvatus
To 9 in. (23 cm)

Pileated Woodpecker
Dryocopus pileatus
To 13 in. (33 cm)
Note large size.

Northern Flicker
Colaptes auratus
To 14 in. (33 cm)
Wing and tail
linings are red.

Calliope Hummingbird
Selasphorus calliope
To 3.5 in. (9 cm)

Rufous Hummingbird
Selasphorus rufus
To 3.5 in. (9 cm)

California Gull
Larus californicus
To 23 in. (58 cm)

Western Wood-Pewee
Contopus sordidulus
To 7 in. (18 cm)
Note 2 narrow
white wing bars.

Mountain Chickadee
Poecile gambeli
To 6 in. (15 cm)

White-breasted Nuthatch
Sitta carolinensis
To 6 in. (15 cm)

Violet-green Swallow
Tachycineta thalassina
To 6 in. (15 cm)

Red-breasted Nuthatch
Sitta canadensis
To 4.5 in. (11 cm)

Mountain Bluebird
Sialia currucoides
To 7 in. (18 cm)

Hermit Thrush
Catharus guttatus
To 7 in. (18 cm)
Note rusty tail
and spotted breast.

Steller's Jay
Cyanocitta stelleri
To 14 in. (35 cm)

American Robin
Turdus migratorius
To 11 in. (28 cm)

Woodhouse's Scrub-Jay
Aphelocoma woodhouseii
To 13 in. (33 cm)

Common Raven
Corvus corax
To 27 in. (68 cm)
Call is a hoarse croak.

Brewer's Blackbird
Euphagus cyanocephalus
To 9 in. (23 cm)

Ruby-crowned Kinglet
Regulus calendula
To 4 in. (10 cm)

American Dipper
Cinclus mexicanus
To 6 in. (15 cm)
Aquatic songbird is
found near clear-
running streams.

Brown Creeper
Certhia americana
To 5 in. (13 cm)
Note downcurved
bill. Forages for
insects on tree
trunks.

Belted Kingfisher
Megaceryle alcyon
To 14 in. (35 cm)

Townsend's Solitaire
Myadestes townsendi
To 8 in. (20 cm)
Note white
eye ring.

Clark's Nutcracker
Nucifraga columbiana
To 13 in. (33 cm)

Dark-eyed Junco
Junco hyemalis
To 7 in. (18 cm)

Bullock's Oriole
Icterus bullockii
To 8 in. (20 cm)

White-crowned Sparrow
Zonotrichia leucophrys
To 8 in. (20 cm)

Black-headed Grosbeak
Pheucticus melanocephalus
To 8 in. (20 cm)

Song Sparrow
Melospiza melodia
To 7 in. (18 cm)
Note central breast spot.

Pine Siskin
Spinus pinus
To 5 in. (13 cm)

Western Tanager
Piranga ludoviciana
To 7 in. (18 cm)

Spotted Towhee
Pipilo maculatus
To 9 in. (23 cm)
Cheerful song is –
drink-your-tea or drink-tea.

Cassin's Finch
Haemorhous cassinii
To 6 in. (15 cm)
Male has a
bright red cap.

Big Brown Bat
Eptesicus fuscus
To 5 in. (13 cm)

Virginia Opossum
Didelphis virginiana
To 40 in. (1 m)
Note long fur and naked tail.

Hoary Bat
Lasiurus cinereus
To 6 in. (15 cm)
Brown fur is
white-tipped.

Snowshoe Hare
Lepus americanus To 20 in. (50 cm)
Coat is white in winter.

Summer   Winter

White-tailed Jackrabbit
Lepus townsendii
To 26 in. (65 cm)
Note large ears
and white tail.

American Pika
Ochotona princeps
To 9 in. (23 cm)
Inhabits rock piles in
mountainous areas.

Montane Vole
Microtus montanus
To 7 in. (18 cm)

Vagrant Shrew
Sorex vagrans
To 4.5 in. (11 cm)

Bushy-tailed Woodrat
Neotoma cinerea
To 18 in. (45 cm)

Deer Mouse
Peromyscus maniculatus
To 8 in. (20 cm)
Has white belly
and a hairy tail.

Western Gray Squirrel
Sciurus griseus
To 23 in. (58 cm)

Golden-mantled Ground Squirrel
Callospermophilus lateralis
To 12 in. (30 cm)

Douglas' Squirrel
Tamiasciurus douglasii
To 14 in. (35 cm)
Also known as chickaree.

California Ground Squirrel
Otospermophilus beecheyi
To 20 in. (50 cm)

Northern Flying Squirrel
Glaucomys sabrinus
To 14 in. (35 cm)

Yellow-pine Chipmunk
Tamias amoenus
To 10 in. (25 cm)
Note yellowish tail.

Lodgepole Chipmunk
Tamias speciosus
To 10 in. (25 cm)
Note rusty sides.

American Badger
Taxidea taxus
To 35 in. (88 cm)

Wolverine
Gulo gulo
To 44 in. (1.1 m)

Common Muskrat
Ondatra zibethicus
To 2 ft. (60 cm)
Aquatic rodent has
a naked tail that is
flattened on its sides.

American Beaver
Castor canadensis
To 4 ft. (1.2 m)

Ringtail
Bassariscus astutus
To 30 in.
(75 cm)

Yellow-bellied Marmot
Marmota flaviventris
To 28 in. (70 cm)

Northern River Otter
Lontra canadensis
To 52 in.
(1.3 m)

Long-tailed Weasel
Mustela frenata
To 21 in. (53 cm)
Note brown feet and
yellowish neck.

Short-tailed Weasel
Mustela erminea
To 13 in. (33 cm)
Note white feet.
Coat is white in
winter except for
black tail tip.

Mink
Neovison vison
To 28 in. (70 cm)
Chin is white.

American Marten
Martes americana
To 26 in. (65 cm)

Western Spotted Skunk
Spilogale gracilis To 19 in. (48 cm)

Common Raccoon
Procyon lotor
To 40 in. (1 m)

Striped Skunk
Mephitis mephitis To 32 in. (80 cm)

Common Porcupine
Erethizon dorsatum
To 3 ft. (90 cm)

Mountain Lion
Puma concolor To 9 ft. (2.7 m)

Bobcat
Lynx rufus
To 4 ft. (1.2 m)

Common Gray Fox
Urocyon cinereoargenteus
To 3.5 ft. (1.1 m)

Bighorn Sheep
Ovis canadensis
To 6 ft. (1.8 m)

Coyote
Canis latrans
To 52 in. (1.3 m)
Note bushy,
black-tipped tail.

Mule Deer
Odocoileus hemionus
To 7.5 ft. (2.3 m)
Rope-like tail is
black-tipped.

Black Bear
Ursus americanus
To 6 ft. (1.8 m)